A Journey to Your Heart

The Greater Truths of
Dr. James Martin Peebles

A Journey to Your Heart

The Greater Truths of
Dr. James Martin Peebles

Virginia L. Harford

A Journey to Your Heart was written by Virginia Harford, who spoke to the great spirit known as Dr. James Martin Peebles through a number of Channels.

ISBN: 978-1-929995-07-3

Publisher: Virginia Harford

Cover image: *A Soul surrendering to the Heart*
          Painting by Celeste, *Visionary Artist*
          e-mail: celeste@spiritsite.net
          http://www.spiritsite.net/celeste

Photographs: Virginia L. Harford

Book design: Patricia Garcia Arreola

This small book is
lovingly dedicated to

Dr. James Martin Peebles
1822–1922

Table of Contents

List of Photos

* Prize-winning photos in *Saturday Review Magazine*

A Prologue

The first time I experienced James Martin Peebles was in the 1990s. A friend suggested we go to an open session with him.

The day was warm and friendly, just one of those start-of-the-summer days in the red-rock Camelot that is the Sedona, Arizona area. A small, unassuming frame house in the Village of Oak Creek, a whisper away from Bell Rock, lord of the Sedona tourist world, was the stage set for the open session with Dr. Peebles.

Dr. James Martin Peebles was born in Vermont in 1822. When he died, he was just days short of one hundred years old. Now James Martin Peebles serves among us as a guiding presence from another place, sharing the mysteries of eternal truths through a chain of trance-mediums around the world.

On this day in this little house, James Martin Peebles was to open a new chapter—this time playing the central role in a story that would point my life in a new direction.

On stage was the Channel. Superficially, trance-mediums I have seen over the years are as varied as the face of nature. They might be male or female, young, old, all sizes, shapes and colors. But all are stamped with the same mystic gift: the ability to surrender their beings to become conduits for messages from the spirit world.

Finally, the cast was to be rounded out by ten "travelers"—listeners, really, who would come to the session to offer not only their presence as witnesses but to make contact with Dr. Peebles on personal matters.

My friend and I were first to arrive. She had an appointment and was anxious to leave right after we received our messages from Dr. Peebles.

Placed around the nondescript little room was a circle of chairs for the ten people expected. At one end of the room a big easy chair was occupied by the Channel. Beside it was a table set with a glass of water and a cassette recorder/player.

At these open sessions the participants usually were able to ask the Spirit just a question or two. At private sessions, however, which normally lasted one hour or so, questions could be asked to one's heart's content.

We took the two chairs to the left of the Channel so that we would be the first called.

The surprise of the day came at that point, because it began to look like we would be the only ones attending the session—a most unusual development. But the time of year—first taste of summer, as it was, with school out, the heat rising in Arizona's red-rock country, and the lazy days of vacation time flooding the calendar—could be suspected of sabotaging the turnout. And it did.

We waited for arrivals to fill the empty chairs. I checked my list of questions. My friend sat in meditative silence. A few minutes passed. Nothing. Suddenly, the Channel said: "I feel Dr. Peebles around."

The Channel's eyes closed. And sitting quietly, from that slim body came a booming voice. It reverberated through the room:

"God bless you, indeed! Dr. Peebles here! It is a joy and a blessing when man and spirit join together in search of the greater truths and awareness."

The force of Spirit was with us, unseen, yet a dynamic presence; heard and felt as if James Martin Peebles himself had materialized in that newborn instant we had snatched from Time itself.

It was a breathless moment. And it was unique—always the same, too, wherever and whenever one entered the process of trance channeling. Many a cynic or skeptic has come from the mystic voyage of a trance-channeling session asking more questions than they arrived with, unsure of previous positions, feeling they were on shifting ground, not terra firma, at all.

I sampled my first trance-channel session in the winter of 1980 in Sedona. Since then, I have taken nearly forty sessions with Dr. Peebles alone.

This little volume, however, is neither tribute nor critique. Trance channeling stands on its own feet. The book is about Spirit, process and message. The matter of order we leave to each of us.

What's before you is a rendezvous with what has been called many things: fate, kismet, destiny. I had no conscious plan to become a "voice"—through the printed word or any other means—for James Martin Peebles. I did not plan to attend an open trance-channeling with Dr. Peebles that day in Sedona. It just happened. I believe this is the way that much of what we know and are takes place.

In the spring, I was working on *Healing Wisdom*, a book on self-help techniques. Dr. Peebles had been providing me with insights for this work. I compiled about forty pages of his Greater Truths with the idea to put this section at the end of *Healing Wisdom*.

But the material from Dr. Peebles kept expanding. It inspired me to realize that it deserved a life of its own. I began a new manuscript, calling it *A Journey to Your Heart*, and worked on both manuscripts simultaneously.

More and more, *A Journey to Your Heart* dominated my thinking and energy. I was completely fascinated by the material. I felt enriched and comforted by the Greater Truths themselves, their seemingly endless turns, depths, values and, above all, wisdom.

If this were so with me, I felt, why couldn't it touch the same chord in a multitude of souls who also needed comfort, nurturing and enrichment from the Spirit world.

I turned full attention to *A Journey to Your Heart*. The book *Healing Wisdom*, which had been my principal work for four years, went to the back burner. Not abandoned, not forgotten, just on a siding until the "Express" came through.

At the end of spring, the Channel decided to set aside trance channeling for a period of time. Another Channel started to channel Dr. Peebles.

I was well underway with *A Journey*. It was crucial that I continue to receive input from Dr. Peebles.

I contacted the second Channel for an appointment to talk with Dr. Peebles by phone. In this arrangement, we have a virtual conference call: the trance Channel and myself on Earth and James Martin Peebles coming to us from the other side.

Almost a year after my first session with Dr. Peebles, a telephone channel session through the second Channel took place.

I told Dr. Peebles I was doing a book on his Greater Truths. He said: "We know. God bless you, indeed!"

As the weeks and months of the calendar flipped away, the relationship between Spirit and me ripened flawlessly, without stress or strain. He advised, counseled, guided. He knew more about me than I did, and on many levels. He knew what I was thinking before the thought could be expressed.

At the very first session in Sedona, I said to Dr. Peebles: "I'm Virginia." "Yes, we know," he said. "Your lower back pain would go away when you put yourself out [start teaching again]."

I was startled. Who at the session knew my background? Only the friend I had come with. But we were there on a whim. I hadn't been teaching T'ai Chi Chih for a while, and now I heard Dr. Peebles chastising me gently about not teaching. I'll say I was startled, and how!

Throughout the many months of contact, the information came in specific, intuitive bites. He was witty and compassionate. I found this source more accurate and helpful than any psychic or general reading I had received before.

A Journey to Your Heart is the discourse from James Martin Peebles recorded at our sessions.

Dr. Peebles' use of the expression "God bless you, indeed!" permeates his conversation with us Earthlings. I once asked him exactly what he meant by that. His response:

"My dear friends. 'God bless you, indeed!' is a way of expressing from the God in you to the God that is the Creator, the God that we all are. It is an acknowledgement between the two. It is an acknowledgment of the All.

"It is all of that, it's all of the gods. It is the Creator, it is you, the creator; it is me, the creator. Do you understand? God bless you, indeed!

"In Thailand they have a ritual where they bow to one another. When they do, it is done in silence but it is saying, 'God bless you, too.' It's an acknowledgment. God bless you, indeed! It starts approximately from the chin to the heart and the hands are folded, not interclasped, but pointing upward." Thus spoke James Martin Peebles.

So God bless you, indeed as you go forth on a journey of surrender to your heart.

**Soul Portrait of Dr. James Martin Peebles
by Celeste, Visionary Artist, Sedona, Arizona**

Foreword

(This is a statement from Dr. Peebles given to Celeste while she was painting his soul portrait.)

I am Dr. Peebles. Physical life is rich with challenges, pain and joy, is it not? I never could get enough of it in spite of the tremendous struggles it entails.

Optimism, intellectual curiosity and the ability to give and receive love are the keys to the kingdom of happiness. Don't think that you can re-create the universe by yourself. Do remember that with God's help, you can create your own appreciation for all that is good in God.

I must admit that my personality as Dr. Peebles was blessed with an optimistic resilience that helped me bounce back from every setback. I used the low times as a springboard to fly higher and further the next time.

Refuse to give in to frustration, guilt or depression. These states of mind are temptations of the flesh in the physical world. We must all contend with them, but we don't have to be conquered by them.

The thing I tried to do in my life as Dr. Peebles was to change the encrusted, buried natural healing within all living things. I wanted to wake people up from their nightmares of disease and death and let them breathe in the joyful richness of life. Even if we experience this unified bliss with nature only once, it is worth all the other unknowing that went before.

So many more now know the truth of eternal life. Progress is being made. I continue to work through physical channels in order to bring about changes in consciousness, since

I couldn't accomplish nearly enough during my lifetime. I persist, probably beyond what is necessary, to serve the human race in any capacity possible. Gigantic strides have been made, but there is still much to accomplish.

In the last century, there was much interest in spiritualism and mediumship. I went to many seances and communicated with the other side. Disillusioned by the silliness and fakery of many of these groups and sensitives, I determined to come back after my death and continue my work.

Now I know how frustrating it can be to guide physical beings from Spirit. It is not so easy to avoid the pitfalls of multidimensional relationships. All have free will and make mistakes. Misuse of power, greed, miscommunications, etc. have a way of interfering in the process no matter how well-intended the parties involved.

I remain an optimist in spite of all the mistakes and misunderstandings. Take the best and leave the rest without condemning the bearer of the gifts. If I can serve you by posing for my portrait, I do so gladly. All of us can get to know each other better.

— Dr. James Martin Peebles
October 1999

Who Was Dr. Peebles?

James Martin Peebles was born in Vermont on March 23, 1822, of Scottish descent. He lived an enviable life on Earth, some might say, dying 36 days short of his 100th birthday and reportedly active to the end. In the near-century he spent on Earth, books were written about him, and he wrote his own books. He was in the diplomatic corps (U. S. Consul in Turkey), hobnobbed with the likes of Mark Twain, made a name for himself as an orator, saw much of the globe and was seen by a biographer as "The Spiritual Pilgrim" when he was just 50. That was only ten years before he became a medical doctor, a calling that gave space and light to his avid interest in the causes of illness and accident and the philosophy behind them. He was married during his time on Earth and raised a family. Contemporaries remembered him as calm and fearless, a man who "listened to the thunder as friend to friend." Reed-like in build, he was tall and some even viewed him as frail. To doubters of the Spiritual force, he winked: "You're all gonna die. You'll have your proof soon enough."

A Journey Begins

✳ ✳ ✳

The trance-medium sat quietly and then her head jerked back and from that slim body a booming voice …

Dawn, Kauai, Hawaii

Three Principles*

※

*G*od bless you indeed, Dr. Peebles here. It is a joy and a blessing when man and spirit join together in search of the greater truths and awareness.

Might we offer encouragement, my dear friends, for your right to give and receive abundance in this, your chosen lifetime. We would like to offer you the following principles to be used as tools in tandem:

1. Loving allowance for ALL things to be in their own time and place, starting with YOURSELF.

2. Increase communication with all of life, starting with YOURSELF, and with respect.

3. Self-responsibility for YOUR life as a creative adventure, for through YOUR choices and perceptions you do indeed create YOUR reality.

My dear friends, you have come to the school called planet Earth to discover and dissolve the illusions of separation within self and between life. Certainly it is your labor of love to diminish these very same illusions wherein you will discover that never in your eternal soul have you been the victim, but always the creator.

---

* The Three Principles are the Creed of James Martin Peebles. These are the usual opening remarks for a private session or for group sessions.

Courthouse Rock, Sedona, Arizona

A Beautiful School
Called Planet Earth

⁂

*M*y dear friends, the process upon planet Earth
is a process of understanding your own hearts,
releasing yourself from the constraints here of your
mind and understanding how to speak the language
of the heart using the mind as a tool rather than an
expression itself.

In order to understand this more fully, my dear friends,
let us take you back, back a bit before you came to planet
Earth, my dear friends. For a moment here, within your
imagination strive to remember a time, my dear friends,
where you were born from the stars. A beautiful and brilliant
light exploded in front of you, God bless you, indeed. There
was a tremendous amount of velocity here as you birthed
forth as a beautiful spirit feeling incredible, tremendous
freedom with a vast and wonderful universe ahead of you.
God bless you, indeed.

My dear friends, it was there that you flew, it was here
that you were free, it was there you had wings, it was there
that you trusted everything and everyone. Until one day, my
dear friends, you found a place within the universe that was
dark, and it was scary. You did not understand it, and you
felt that perhaps within this darkness there was an absence,
that there was no God anymore.

With that thought, my dear friends, you began to enter into a consciousness that brought you to planet Earth for the very first time. Your beautiful guides, friends and family were helping you to understand your consciousness, that which is in touch with God, my dear friends, that which is your enlightened and beautiful heart.

I n order to explore this, your guides have created a beautiful school, they said, a beautiful school called planet Earth. It looks rather amazing from a distance, a beautiful blue orb here floating out in the universe, out in the center of this darkness.

And what is this, a beautiful gem for all to hold in their hands, God bless you, indeed? As you move closer, you cannot help it. You want that beauty, that light, that wonder that you see there upon this Earth. You move closer and closer to it, embracing it with love, embracing it with clarity. "Ah yes, I did understand, after all, there is light in the darkness." God bless you, indeed.

As you move closer and closer to this very beautiful, mystical orb in the universe, as you get closer, my dear friends, and you enter the atmosphere, something begins to change, and it is not just a beautiful blue orb. It is certainly, my dear friends, much richer than that—and you begin to see a fuller spectrum of light. You begin to see color, and you begin to see brilliant colors—of green, of brown, of golden flowers, of beautiful chirping birds in red and yellow and green. And, God bless you, indeed, goodness gracious, it is so beautiful, you come closer and closer still. This is magnificent—more light and color than you ever imagined could exist there in the darkness.

G od bless you, indeed, you come closer and closer, and as you do, you begin to pass through an area called the Valley of Forgetfulness, where you forget where you were in the universe.

You forget times of old and you focus entirely, 100 percent, upon this beautiful planet Earth. And you do so willingly because you love it so very much. You don't want to be separate from it at all. And yet as you come closer and closer still, you begin to see life and movement and separation. You begin to see a sense of self here, one that feels separate.

And God bless you, indeed, my dear friends, it is here that you land upon the Earth with quite a thud. Everything suddenly is rather heavy. Your heart begins to drop, too, and you wonder, "What is this planet Earth? Have I been tricked here? You see, I told you the darkness was something to fear, and somebody tricked me as I came to this planet Earth."

But my dear friends, there are a few things here upon this Earth. They don't feel like tricks, and they feel rather nice, the soft earth between your toes. Suddenly you are seeing a stranger peeking out from behind a bush, and you fall in love. You come closer still and say, "Ah yes, perhaps I was wrong. Perhaps this planet Earth is not so bad after all." And you touch hands and you mingle words and you strive to understand each other in a state of intimacy and ecstasy there within the physical.

Yet, my dear friends, something then occurs and you realize that there are differences here and these differences feel like violence to you. And it frightens you. Again you back away, feeling that you have been tricked once again. And so it continues for all of you as you journey to the Earth. Some of you in your very first lives chose to leave almost immediately because it was rather overwhelming. Yet from a distance you saw the beautiful blue orb and thought perhaps there would be another opportunity there that you did not see.

What you find time and time again, coming back over and over again is that you can't help but be attracted to the richness, the diversity, the dynamics, the wondrous qualities of planet Earth. And you begin to fall in love with more and more aspects of the very same.

Y ou begin to realize how you are a part of this Earth, how every thought, every deed that you create here has a resonance. And, my dear friends, the only purpose for you upon the Earth is to immerse yourself in life.

You ask others to bring their hearts to the surface, to change, to survive, to win their battles. Now you will begin to turn within. Ask yourself to come to the surface, to speak your truth, to bring your heart to the world. It is there that the world finds color and richness and life and light. It is there that you will bring God forward.

Y ou, my dear friends, are the paintbrush. Planet Earth is your canvas. And your heart that comes from God, my dear friends, is the paint with which you color it.

My dear friends, you are all very beautiful spirits, and now that you are here fully and completely upon planet

Earth, feel your feet, wiggle your toes for a moment here. Feel yourself within your beautiful, beautiful bodies. Feel your consciousness, give thanks for this beautiful consciousness. Commit to yourself now that deep within your heart, your greatest desire is to bring yourself to the surface with richness, with all your diversity, all your dynamics. Because all is in its present essence when you no longer deny yourself, when you no longer struggle with shame, with guilt, etc.

All of that is a labor of love that you give to the world as a service: to mankind, to God, to the universe. You touch so many without even having to leave your homes. Bring that to the surface which is you, and that in its purest essence, is Divinity, is love.

Journey to Your Heart

✳

It is here, my dear friends, that you will experience planet Earth as a place where you may dance as you journey to your own heart.

Life is a dance, my dear friends. Everything that occurs around you has value, has purpose. There is not one single solitary bit of life here upon Earth that you would ever want to push away.

We are going to be in a deepening process of understanding how to reduce your arm's length with the world around you, to understand and explore that this consciousness upon Earth is an experiment—and it is understanding the value of your heart, of you, my dear friends. It is here where you begin to turn the clock back, because you fall into a state of love, a condition wherein you understand that ...

...the learning never ever ends; it spirals out now and forevermore, and it is there that you continue in an ongoing exploration of God.

We, too, are embarking upon the journey each and every moment. It is a wondrous state of being in which we exist. And we are here to help you and to guide you into your enlightenment, my dear friends.

W *hen you cross the threshold, it is there that you feel consciousness of love for everything and everyone.*

You find value and purpose in patience as well as in anger. And it is here that you will no longer feel tired, because you will no longer be resisting anything that comes from within you. You will find it is all right to bring your passion to the surface.

Write down the word passion, and think about the multidimensional meaning of passion in the universe. There is sexual passion, there is verbal passion, there is emotional passion, there is the passion of sitting in silence, there is the passion of waiting, there is the passion of discovery, there is the passion of adventure, the passion of courage, there is the passion, my dear friends, that comes from immersing yourself in sadness, in the tears, in the melancholy and in the misunderstandings, in the deceptions and in the lies, in the belief systems that are not your own as you would think, and in immersing yourselves in individuals that look different from you, in embracing them when their arms do not feel good around your body.

M *y dear friends, there is passion to be found in every single solitary corner of the universe.*

And from our perspective, when you understand that the basis of this passion is love, it is there that you find forgiveness, forgiveness for yourself, forgiveness for others and, my dear friends, for God.

Because it is there that you are no longer pushing any part away, understanding that all of it is you and you are all of it. You begin to understand how you create this echo of self into life, my dear friends, ...

...and how life is so beautiful because it provides you with a basis of understanding the honest echo that you receive in return.

As you are adventuring here, you begin to understand the richness, the diversity, the quality of life that you seek. It is one where you can feel truly nourished, truly find value in every single, solitary moment. Ask for our help and we will be there, alongside you while you explore the Three Principles.

We speak to you with the language of love, God bless you, indeed, that comes from the heart. As you begin to understand how you receive, you can't do it with your mind, because your mind is always creating stresses of second-guessing this relationship.

B ut, my dear friends, fall in love with your heart. Journey therein and you will find contact there, and it will continue and spiral out forevermore, God bless you, indeed.

A way to get in contact with your heart is to place your hand over your heart and tap, tap, tap on your chest, chest, chest. And you say to yourself over and over, "Heart, teach my mind today. Heart, teach my mind today."

T apping your chest, you can say that a few ways. "Teach my mind today, heart. Teach my mind today, heart. Teach my mind today, heart. Today, heart, teach my mind."

As you say it and repeat it over and over, my dear friends, as rapidly as you can, tapping your chest, the words will run together, and it is here you will begin to release, to relax and to unwind.

Swan, Vista, California

Opening Your Heart

❊

When you do some exercises for opening the heart, this automatically helps with the aging process.

*Y*ou can sit each day and make a list of all the things you are grateful for and feel them within your heart.

And when you talk to people, speak from your heart.

*T*ake big deep breaths each day, my dear friends, and breathe deeply. And as you breathe in life and you breathe out, you release all that does not belong there.

Do you understand? These all help to open the heart. And you can also imagine a big zipper and that on these seven layers you just pretend you're opening the zipper and go through and pull back all the shades. Do you understand how that might be done? This definitely has an effect on the energy fields of the heart.

VH: Would you clarify a little more about the zipper?
God bless you, indeed. We were using that as an example that the heart is like a zipper. As you open it up, the magic begins to appear. Much the same as if you have a jacket, my dear, and you unzip it, then more is exposed. Correct? That

15

is what we were addressing. As you unzip the heart, more can be exposed as to who you are.

Bell Rock, Sedona, Arizona

Mother Earth

✳

Many desire to widen and broaden their scope of under-standing of this beautiful blue orb called planet Earth. And certainly it is here that you will be helping her along in correcting a few things.

You can focus your attention and love upon Mother Earth, your awareness of planet Earth. As you step upon her, you give her love and understand that you put your resonance into her.

Certainly there are a few storms coming up in the weeks and months ahead, and certainly other occurrences upon planet Earth.

Everything is fine, my dear friends, nothing to fear, but to understand it is certainly a process whereby planet Earth is moving into a new dimension, a greater frequency.

And it is here each and every one of you is being asked to understand your hearts with greater awareness, certainly surrendering there, certainly through a state of deeper and deeper compassion. God bless you, indeed.

My dear friends, as you deepen your own compassion within your heart and soul, it is there where you will find a very beautiful kiss of life and understanding from God, my dear friends.

C *ertainly God that you are, for you are God and God is you.*

And certainly it is here, my dear friends, this is a difficult concept to embrace at times But understand that throughout your life here on planet Earth, at times you fear judgment and at times you want to feel the arm's length and distance from the world around you.

But, God bless you, indeed, once again you come back together through courses here of dynamics, of diversity, adversity, etc.

A *nd it is here that you deepen your awareness of self in relationship to life as you learn to embrace all the extremes and the extension of self, God bless you, indeed, and all the spectrums of light and life within you, my dear friends.*

And so everyone upon the planet Earth will be asked and whispered secrets in the night, if you will, within their hearts. Certainly it is here that everyone is being asked to deepen their compassion upon planet Earth.

Earth Changes

✳

You are certainly worthy of growth and attention and movement here upon planet Earth. There is certainly much to explore, etc. For everyone, from our perspective, to abandon your dreams is to abandon your heart. To try, my dear friends, to place expectation on how the future is going to be formed, we would not even attempt this ourselves because everything can change in an instant.

We can share with you that down the road a piece such-and-such is going to happen because at the time, everything is in proper place for it to occur in this fashion. But it can change; there is free will.

A nd you do have the capability of changing and transforming the energy of planet Earth, of changing what you see as the possible end of the world, if you will.

God bless you, indeed. You keep the world alive through your dreams, through your heart, bringing and expressing it on the surface, through the attention that you give to the world.

This is a part of why we ask at the very outset here that everyone, in the weeks ahead as you walk upon the planet Earth, remember that there is a beating heart there within her and give your love and attention to Mother Earth, God bless you, indeed. For this in indeed your home, and there are many rooms upon it, etc.

So, my dear friends, certainly we would ask that you take a little vacation within yourself and allow yourself your imaginings, your wonderings about your future. You can write it down on a piece of paper if you like, as for it all to happen because you, my dear friends, inspire it to be so. You do have that kind of power within you, you understand? As does everyone here.

You are beautiful spirits—each and every one—a family here upon planet Earth. This is a time of change. Certainly, my dear friends, rather than feeling panic, find luxury in this change.

I t is a time of growth and opportunity for everyone, unimaginable opportunity for expression of compassion, expression of your individuality.

Everyone is going to be called upon to understand their heart's desire as well, and to bring it to the surface and speak it to the world. Because certainly the world is requiring it now as it moves into a new dimension.

There is going to be tremendous upheaval, but a wonderful experience for all. Certainly for the courageous adventurers that you are, you want to journey with it, not against it. You can't stop change, my dear friends, it's going to happen anyway, so celebrate it, surrender to it. In an expression of your own vulnerability, you find that you are wiser. You find it is a more magical experience here upon planet Earth, God bless you indeed. You're beautiful spirits, my dear friends.

Honoring Yourself

✳

Everything will go a little easier if you take just a couple of small steps to honor yourself each and every day. Sometimes the recreation that you are requiring is just a little silence. Meditation, my dear friends, is simply a requirement for you to have some silence, some space for yourself to sit and allow yourself to relax, to slow down just a little more.

*L*et go of the "there" to get to, and simply surrender to your heart. That is where you will create movement in your life.

Movement is coming in contact with your heart's desire— what you want, what you choose, what you want to create now in terms of the world around you, in terms of creating magic, new settings, certainly changing external environments.

But it first starts within you. The environment does not change first. You create that movement within yourself simply through a choice, through a perception, through an idea. But this, my dear friends, is contact with your heart, with your heart's desire, surrendering more and more to this, to your own will.

*A*nd you will find you are surrendering to the will of the universe. That is what is for your highest good

Dancers, Guadalajara, Jalisco, Mexico

Fatigue

❋

VH: **What can people do to help overcome fatigue?**

Well, my dear, things that would help people with fatigue, we could start with a life adjustment, as we well know that goes without saying.

M ost fatigue is because people are not honoring themselves and they are not taking time to do what makes their hearts sing …

…and so they get more and more tired, as they see no way out of it. This creates many effects that play upon the body, and it creates the outcome of fatigue and the stress syndrome that everybody talks about.

Cathedral Rock, Sedona, Arizona

Soul and Spirit

✴

VH: On the Earth, there is a lot of discussion between the soul and the spirit in a person. Would you comment?

Well, the spirit of a person is not so different from the soul as we look upon it. You have a human being, and within the human being there is soul as they say and that adds substance to it.

VH: Is soul individualized?

God bless you, indeed. Yes, but so is spirit. When you pass from this Earth plane, we would refer to Virginia on the other side as spirit, would we not? But when she was in human form, we would say, "She's a delightful soul."

VH: So they are interchangeable?

Interchangeable, yes. Often times though, within the human form, you refer more to them as, "She has a sweet soul, a sweet essence about her." It's not always thought of as being more spirit. They are interchangeable, my dear, but man has divided it up a bit differently. So when you are on the other side, you refer to them more as spirits. It's like once they leave their body, then they become spirit. But, my dear, within that spirit is a soul, too. They are all the same, but because of the human form they more or less refer to the soul as being the spirit. Do you understand what we are saying?

VH: Somewhat.

Okay. Within you, if Coco here were speaking about you, she would say, "She has a good soul." But it is the same as your spirit. But it is in human form, so it is like two pieces coming together. So you have your spirit inside your human body and we will refer to that as your soul. Do you understand? So when you pass to the other side, then people tend not to understand that it's the same, but they will refer to you as spirit. But actually, my dear, they are the same.

❋

Life Purpose

❊

VH: So many people are concerned about what their life purpose is. Please comment on this.

Well, we can comment on that in a nutshell, but you probably want more. Life purpose, my dear, is to master oneself, to claim the Divinity you are, to dissolve the illusion of separation.

Now, what happens along the path of life? You see many trails you decide to take and explore, and all of that, my dear, helps feed into discovering who you are.

You may want to be an artist in this lifetime, so you explore the path of art. You want to be a truck driver, so you explore that.

B ut, my dear, truly it is about becoming the God you are and dissolving the illusion of separation. When you dissolve the illusion of separation and become the best you can be, it sets up a chain reaction within the universe for others to do the same.

What we say is, for the Channel, whom you know so well to be the best trance medium she can be, what must she do? Or the other Channel? What is it they must do? God bless you, indeed. They must become the best they know how to be. They cannot go out and tell somebody else how to be the best they can be.

So it is you focusing on you. That is the purpose of life, my dear. Sometimes the simplest of all answers are the most difficult to understand.

Children near Tokyo, Japan

Touching

❋

VH: *I have read of the importance of touch in our lives. Will you please comment on it.*

Touch is so very important, my dear. When you are touched, one God is touching the next God and through that, healing occurs. So without touch, life does not survive.

If you have high blood pressure, it diminishes through touch. In aggravated souls, the nerves are diminished through touching. Through touch and opening the heart, almost all illnesses, my dear friends, would not exist.

There are many things that man does not know about as far as how deeply this goes. It is soul touching soul. It is memory touching memory when we were all as One ...

... and dissolving the illusion of separation. So touching encompasses everything there is to life and more, my dear friends.

VH: I'm reading a book called Conversations With God, Book 3. Are most of the things in that book true?

God bless you, indeed. Very inspired, my dear, and yes, right on! God bless you, indeed.

The author is a beautiful being, and yes, my dear, he truly was having a conversation with God. It has done much to help the planet, to open mankind's awareness and to dissolve the illusion of separation that a mere mortal could have a conversation with God. My, my!

So it does away with the pedestal upon which the great ascended masters and God have been placed, my dear friends, for we are all Gods and we are all One.

Energy Fields

❊

VH: Will you comment on the energy fields of the body.

There are seven different layers on the outside of the human body. The body responds to energy. An example is how electricity travels through a power line to the light bulb from the power source.

*W*e are connected to a divine power source, and it travels through the different layers of our etheric bodies and to our human body and circulates around our body.

We have frequencies, and the body operates off these frequencies in the energy fields around us, the seven layers of the human body, which are the seven layers of the etheric body.

What we are addressing is that all of the planet is energy. It is not to say that a lamp is anything less than—it is molecules—it is energy vibrating at a slower frequency. Everything is energy. Everything has a Divine order to it. What we were addressing too is changing the mind set to think that energy is invisible, energy can slow down so it creates form. Energy can speed up which creates non-form. But in reality, all is energy. Thoughts are energy. Human form is energy.

Thoughts do create instantly—energy forms. So you think a thought, but the slightest thought in an unkind way creates an energy form of that thought wave. Because, again, don't forget you are a creator, you are a God. Therefore, everything that you do creates. Yes, at different rates.

Woman in Church, Central Mexico

Religion

✳

VH: I believe all paths lead to God. Is this true?

It is true, my dear, that all religions are like paths leading to God in the center.

There is no such thing as "the" religion, for all religions have truth, and as long as a religion teaches Divine love, it is the right path for that being.

Some religions feel they are the only one because ego is still mixed in, my dear. It doesn't mean that they don't have truths, but they are fearful that if they don't hold all people to themselves, these beings will walk away and join another church. Then what would they do for a livelihood?

Montezuma's Castle, Camp Verde, Arizona

The Concept of Time

✵

VH: Time seems to be changing all the time. Will you please help me understand?

It is very difficult to explain, but we will do the best we can. Time does not really exist, for past, present, and future are all together in one ball.

You are in a place where time is passing fast, and you think, "Where did it go? I just looked at the clock a minute ago and it was 1:00 o'clock, and now it is 5:00 o'clock." It's like being lost someplace. Then in another time period, you look at the clock and it is 1:00 o'clock. You look at the clock again and it is 1:01. You look at the clock again and it's only 1:05! You think, "Is it ever going to speed up?"

That's because time is currently changing. The clocks are not the same as they once were on the same calendar of events. It is because of the speedup of the planet and the transformations that are taking place. So at one instant it can be fast, and in the next extremely slow, because realities are beginning to merge together.

A change in time is setting things on course. You've also heard about the magnetic pole exchange, where there is no north and south. The planet is making shifts in that way, and there is a change in time affecting that.

So actually, my dear, there is no such thing as time. It is only something we created as a means of telling us how it's going to go. If you go on vacation and throw away the clock, everything still gets accomplished, but you're not trying to do it by a certain time—you go by feeling!

❊

Shoemaker, Guadalajara, Jalisco, Mexico

Aging

VH: I have thought about aging, and I wonder what we can do about it?

*I*n thinking about aging, my dear friends, you don't get older unless you choose to get older.

Change the way you view aging and realize, my dear friends, that you are not aging, but buying into a belief structure of having to grow older, etc. Do you understand? This is not something you have to take part in.

You can say each day, "I am younger and younger and feeling better and better."

When you do some exercises for opening the heart, this automatically helps with the aging process.

VH: Please comment about what would help people accept the aging process?

Well, my dear, from our perspective, there really does not have to be aging. It is only a mind set, an illusion that all have come together to create that they must age because that is what is said. However, you do not have to age if you choose.

If you would come together and want to change the dream, you can say, "Well, we're going to stay at the age of thirty and never grow any older."

You may be upon the planet Earth ninety years, but you don't have to have the body age with that. Do you understand? It can stay however you choose to have it. You are the creator, you are the God.

❋

Bride and Groom, Oregon

Relationships

※

VH: *Please comment on relationships, an area that we all are so interested in.*

Relationships—that is truly a large subject. Really, my dear friends, if you come to the school called planet Earth and wish to have a relationship that mirrors nothing to you, then why be in one? So relationships from the onset were not designed, my dear friends, to be smooth and without bumps in the road. They are there to teach, as a mirror, where one needs to work upon oneself. That is the beautiful dance of the relationship. After you have been in a relationship for some time, it does take changes as the people grow together; it can become a much smoother dance.

The relationships in the future, my dear friends, will be changing. They will be coming together with a lot more light in them. In the relationships that most people are so concerned with now, they are wondering, "Why isn't everything going smoothly, and why don't I have the feeling I had when I first met this human being?"

Well, my dear friends, relationships weren't designed to be smooth. They were designed to help us perfect ourselves. So it is a bit of a paradox here.

*R*elationships *truly are the dance to your own soul. It is a way to be in touch with all the parts of yourself that you cannot see.*

So it mirrors to you not only the rough, but it mirrors to you the sensitivity, the gentleness, and the love. It is a beautiful dance, much like climbing a ladder together. One partner steps up on the next level of the ladder and reaches down and says, "May I help you?" And through that dance you move up. Then you might go up on the next level and say to your beloved one, "Might I help you?"

But it is truly a dance, my dear friends, and in a dance of any sort there is push and pull. But it is learning to dance in harmony.

*A*nd *through the dance of harmony, you learn to dance in harmony with Spirit. So it is a mirroring of the heavens too within the relationship dance upon the Earth.*

Falling in Love

VH: How can we learn to love another?

God bless you, indeed. You ask about the love that we are seeking to have for another. You do this without judgment and with curiosity.

A nd when you are a seeker of the greater truths, you are a seeker of understanding here, you are a seeker of healing, you are a seeker of compassion, and so on and so forth, my dear friends.

The process of falling in love with a human being here upon planet Earth is no different than the process which most of you experienced in coming to planet Earth, seeing this beautiful blue orb sitting there in the universe, absolutely magnificent.

"What a jewel, what a gem. I want to go forward. I want to discover this beautiful place that I have heard is called planet Earth. It looks magnificent from a distance, absolutely beautiful, serene, confident. There is no problem there. I love it because it is one color. I can understand it from this distance.

"I come a little closer still. Ah, well, perhaps there are a few clouds there upon this planet Earth. That's all right, they're white. They look good to me. It's okay, it fits my concept of what is good and proper and pure. And as I come closer, I see little birdies and other things within the environment, and it becomes a rather chaotic mess. All kinds of colors are sparkling and snapping out at me.

"I land in the middle of a forest, and I find myself there facing a tiger. It jumps at me, startling and frightening me then it bites me and hurts me. Goodness gracious, I am now wrestling with a monster! A monster of diversity, and God bless you, indeed, it is there that I choose to exit."

It is the same within the relationship. Ah, there you see your loved and cherished one from a distance. Your heart is wide open; love is there on the surface. You embrace the beloved entirely into your being. Your beloved is absolutely perfect. You know this to be true; you feel the essence. But as you draw closer to examine, you see all the little imperfections inside that perfection.

And you begin to see where you still have some areas where you are holding life at arm's length, struggling to change what is already perfect.

A nd, God bless you indeed, that is where the struggle begins, my dear. That is where you learn about true love, absolute love.

And this comes from within you, my dear friends. It's your choice as to whether to love someone with all the person's conditions surrounding that. You understand? Even loving the judgment, loving the disharmony, my dear. It is there where you find that there is purpose in all of it.

Thank you for asking about love. It gives us the opportunity to express the greater truths as we understand them. And it is from our hearts that we love to share with your world. If it can move you along your path just a little more, it's our greatest joy. you understand? God bless you, indeed.

Enlightenment

VH: Many people on the spiritual path have questions about enlightenment. Please comment on it.

Enlightenment is when one removes the foggy glasses through which one is looking. My dear friends, it is much as if you were looking through a pair of bifocals, yet you don't need glasses. What is it that you are going to see? You are going to see a different point of view with many clouds in it. When you remove the clouds, all of a sudden you say, "Now I see it as it truly is," and that is an enlightened point of view.

You do that by surrendering, my dear friends. The more you surrender and the more you walk into the darker places, the more enlightened you become. And then you understand there really is no one way of doing it. All ways are correct, all perspectives are correct, and you surrender deeper into the arms of the universe.

With each birthday you are committing to life once again, round and round you go. Goodness gracious, you are absolutely firmly committed inside of yourself to understand this thing called life here upon planet Earth, certainly in terms of your enlightenment. And so you inch your way a little closer in every given moment. But we are going to tell you a secret: It can happen in the blinking of an eye, God bless you, indeed. And certainly it shall when it does occur.

S o let go of any "there" you want to get to and realize that this process you are engaged in, in *terms of surrender, is certainly an awakening of your heart.*

When you allow your heart to speak fully and completely, it is there that you find your enlightenment.

Guanajauto, Mexico

Parallel Universes

❊

VH: *Are there parallel universes?*

God bless you, indeed, there are parallel universes. You can live in parallel universes. It is a choice; you can exist in many places. There are many other planets where you do different things.

Can the river run on both sides of the stream? Do you understand? You have a river, an east bank and a west bank. Is it the same river? Is the water that is on the east the same as the water on the west? It isn't, is it? But it is. Do you see what we are saying?

> *You are only a portion, my dear, of who you really are. You are not all of you, for there are other aspects of you out experiencing different things to bring back to the whole.*

You can ask to remember that while you are here upon the planet. You must ask that the veils be removed. What will happen—it won't happen overnight—ask that they will slowly begin to come down and you will begin to understand and experience parallel worlds.

You will begin to experience what this is really like, and you will have a deeper understanding. You don't have to wait for anything until you pass over, my dear. It is only set up that when you become aware and have the ability to ask, you do the asking. Then it is granted. Remember, my dear, you are the creator.

Fertility Statue Near Morelia, Mexico

Human Sexuality

※

VH: *I have heard much discussion about becoming enlightened through human sexuality. Is this possible?*

I n the relationship of human sexuality to the Divine, yes, certainly you can reach enlightenment upon the planet Earth.

First of all, you are going to have to bridge something there. You are going to have to bridge your fear of intimacy; you are going to have to bridge your belief in separation.

And to truly have a divine experience, you must realize that you and your partner, with whom you are engaging in sexual acts, are engaging in this as one consciousness.

When you are in this divine state of expression of self, the act of human sexuality becomes less physical, my dear, in its expression. Then it becomes a spiritual act where the bodies are just functioning, for example, as an antenna of this energy, very much as the channel here. She steps aside and allows us to come through and use her physical body; she is acting as a transmitter of sorts. You understand?

And so it is the same. Your bodies would be used in this way through human sexuality, to bridge this through orgasm, for example, to experience life as one being. To bridge this takes a tremendous amount of concentration, certainly concentrated breathing, a focus of attention upon the person with whom you are engaged (person or persons, depending upon the situation). From our perspective, one on one is much better because it is more focused. It would be like the channel trying to bring in twenty spirits through her body using one mouth to talk. That would not be an easy task.

B   *ut for ultimate divine satisfaction, if you will, to engage with one person, one individual, one-on-one contact is best.*

Putting your entire focus of attention, all your love, the very best and quickest way to find this cosmic-orgasm state of being, if you will, is during the course of intercourse to gaze into each other's eyes, eyes open. Very difficult for human beings to do this. But as you come to the point of climax, be looking into each other's eyes with great intensity and great focus, no arm's length whatsoever, you will find yourselves falling into each other. It is here that everything explodes in magnificent light, and there is a peacefulness and at the same time an excitement.

It is not felt as much physically, although anyone watching would see that physically there is lots going on, but you would not be as aware of it. And you would fall into a state of bliss, though it be temporary at best because it would be almost akin to an astral-body experience, but you are not in the astral body, you are truly in touch with the divine consciousness of the universe.

W   *hen you come into this state of bliss, my dear, there is no separation between male and female or bad and good or right and wrong. God bless you, indeed. It is all one. It is a state of oneness.*

We understand about bringing through as much of the female sexual energy through the female body as possible, and as much male sexual energy through the male as possible.

But what you are doing truly in divine union, my dear friends, is bringing through the aspect of self. You bring it through with as much enthusiasm as you can muster, as much love as you can muster, and you fall in love with the state of wonder about your partner.

Now mind you, this does not rule out what you would call contact between two women or two men. These are all similar experiences, but going about it a little differently. You understand? That is a whole other arena in itself, but it can happen through various functions.

But from our perspective, once again, there is something to be said about the divine celebration of self, male to female, and through this energy being generated, catapulting into bliss by falling into each other. So you don't want to push the female sexual energy to the surface as a way to keep the male at bay, but rather to create it with enthusiasm, falling in love with wonder at the male sexual energy.

The problems that come about, in terms of human sexuality, come through a belief in arms's length—certainly through thoughts of shame and guilt and so on.

VH: *Do we ever have to give up human sexuality on the earth plane to reach spiritual enlightenment?*

From our perspective here and this is one perspective in the universe, ... we feel we are pretty accurate here, my dear friends, in terms of your own enlightenment, you are working here upon planet Earth as a student of the Divine.

You are working to discover and dissolve the illusions of separation within yourself and between life.

When we speak to you of 'Loving allowance for all things to be …', we mean everything, including you, all sensations, including all feelings, even those things you feel are wrong, inappropriate, ones you prefer would just dehydrate and fall off.

ut my dear friends, you understand that to truly fall in love with the state of oneness, that consciousness, you need to realize in celebration of self that everything exists within you, and that within every man, within every woman and within every child exists an enlightened being.

And, as well, within that enlightenment there also exists a variety of temperaments ranging from happiness to sadness. You have great artists, you have great humanitarians, and you, as well, have the potential, the prospect, of murderer and so on and so forth. So everything exists there, but you choose to bring to the surface, within your enlightenment, my dear, what encompasses everything. And what is that? In your divine state of being, my dear friends, it is summarized by a state, an energy of consciousness and being that is love. So when you are bringing love to the surface, when you are truly celebrating self, that is all you acknowledge.

VH: Is it possible to have an intimate relationship with two different people at the same time?

There is certainly upon planet Earth different courses, different (shall we say) classes here. One class can be the one wherein you find yourself in commitment to one. The reason for this is to refine your perspective there.

I f you can learn to love one person, to see yourself reflected in that person fully, and to learn about yourself; if you can fall in love with the exploration of self in relationship to this person, then you will find your enlightenment, because you are falling in love with "you."

That is the commitment. That is the relationship that you are seeking. Do you understand? Because within that, everything and everyone exists. So when you are in love with yourself, you are having a relationship with all of life, with everything. Ya, absolutely. In answer to your question, however, we didn't quite finish.

In terms of sexual energy and sexual exchange, to refrain from sexual activity because of a belief that you must do thus and so to reach your enlightenment would be an illusion of separation so you are still not within your enlightenment. We cannot tell you to eat carrots on Tuesday, refrain from sex, and so on and so forth and that it is there that you would find your enlightenment, my dear friends. If we would do that, we would be trying to sell you something, and we don't want to do that.

W e want you to explore life, to find yourself in love with everything. Because, my dear, if you can imagine for a moment that you are God ... does God, my dear, push away any of life?

Is God not present everywhere, in everything? Is God not all loving? Is God not all powerful? And so, my dear, does God not forgive everyone beyond your wildest dreams and imaginations? Can you imagine that God would forgive Lucifer, for example? That is how loving God is.

How much love do you want in your life? Do you not want to find and touch the 'Face of God' within your own consciousness? Is that enlightenment, my dear friends? God would not push away anyone or anything. That is a state of love and awareness of self in relationship to life that everything is One. Everything is perfect as is. You understand? God bless you, indeed.

Parallel Lives

✳

VH: I have heard the concept that we live many lives at one time. Please explain.

You exist on the Earth plane, but you also exist in a higher form called your Higher Self. Then there is another aspect of you that exists in another so-called time period.

The "past" was set up by the beings upon planet Earth for this current time called "future." And the future time is another aspect of you, and you are setting things up there, too. Do you understand? As you existed in the past, you exist now and you exist in the future. It is all the same.

When you look at something from a distance away, you can see the whole scope. When you are on an airplane, so to speak, you can see from one side to the other of the whole city, even if it is a very large city.

As you look upon it, you say, "My goodness, when I am in the city, I can't see all this. It takes me an hour and a half to drive from one side to the other. But when I am up here in an airplane, I can see it all with my eyes at once in one shot."

*W*ell, it is as we look upon time, my dear. The past, the present and the future we can see the same as if you were looking at the city from an airplane.

Now, you live in a house smack dab in the center of the city. For you, time exists right there. You also exist on the outskirts of the city both to the north and to the south, but you are not aware of that.

Let's say the south is the past, the middle of the city is you now, and the future is the north. So, my dear, you exist in time past in many of the things you have set up for yourself. As your ancestors, so you speak of, my dear, were you. Just as I, Dr. Peebles, have not had just one lifetime but many, so have you. You have existed in all of these. You evolve and you change, my dear, because each lifetime you learn more.

> *ut it is all occurring at the same time. Because we don't have time like you think of it. The soul evolves quite rapidly upon Earth and your time is only a flicker here.*

So things that are going on in the future are also you and your friends, etc. who are up there in the "future."

It is very difficult to explain. The best analogy we can come up with would be the airplane!

Anger

※

VH: *Please comment on anger.*

Anger is a tragic expression of an unmet need. It is something you're wanting in life, something to be given to you. You feel that you have that right, so why aren't they meeting your requirements? In reality, my dear friends, it is you that is the Creator. It is about you not having met your own needs. That is basically about anger in a nutshell.

It is an expression. So when you see somebody in great anger, you know they are in pain and have a need that has not been met. Most beings are not aware that it is their job. This is why they are feeling this, in order to meet their need. And once they do meet their need, they no longer have the anger. But anger is a way to get in touch with this. It is a way to manifest it outwardly so they can see it.

Anger is a movement, an expression, and through expressing it, what happens? You see, "Oh, this is an unmet need that I have buried very deep within me."

*Y*ou begin to understand that anger is a force that creates movement within your life.

When you are feeling anger, but all wrapped up in concerns as to whether or not to express it or feel it or put it at arm's length or embrace it, etc., it creates disturbances and can respond as depression. This is immobility that is essentially inside, but it truly is a point of hibernation. Then at long last, anger does come to the surface.

Much of life has taught us that to have the emotion of anger is bad. Not that there is a bad—you know that. But it is an expression that is not looked upon kindly.

B̶ut indeed, my dear friends, anger is a momentum, a force, getting out of an energy that has trapped a thought process within you where you felt you had no say.

So truly it is the expression of an unmet need. But when it comes out, it helps you identify it and understand what it is that is needing attention. Without the movement of the anger, you would not be able to see this. From our perspective, we see anger as a wonderful tool.

Illness

✳

What happens when you get an illness? The attention is centered on you. There are so many possibilities and opportunities here within our wonderful herbs. And certainly, as you suspect here, my dear friends, absolutely everything is curable through your food sources. And you can also take these food sources all day long, weeks and months and years, and get nowhere. And why would that be?

*B*ecause, my dear friends, the balance that you truly seek is within your own spirit, within your own soul.

So if you don't stop walking a certain walk with anger, you will begin to find that imbalances in the body will take over regardless of your medicines. You can cut off that part of your body, but you still feel the pain. So never forget, my dear friends, that the spiritual processes and the functioning of your awareness here—part of why you experience ill health—is simply to get you to slow down a little bit more, to fall in love deeper with yourself.

You can run around like a chicken with its head cut off (what a horrible thing to use as an analogy here, but it does work). And, God bless you, indeed, my dear friends, you will find that the moment you get sick, there is nothing more important than honoring yourself. You understand? Suddenly you love yourself very much, "Pity poor me. Look at this. Where is everyone? Why aren't they here to rub my feet and my temples and bring me my tea, and to take care of me." Isn't that a silly way to be?

VH: Yes, I have heard that if we would only stop and do what we do when we get sick before we get sick, then we would not get sick!

Precisely on the other hand, my dear, you want a cure for the common cold? One day a month if you ask someone to wait on you hand and foot and you relish in it and do it with sincerity from the heart, you will not get sick. It has to be absolutely without shame or guilt. Here I am today, honor me. Ya? And isn't that wonderful in your life if you would take one day for this sort of honoring of self, within your year, that adds up to twelve days a year, and this takes precedence over all the rest.

Healing

❋

VH: I would like to understand how we heal.

Y ou keep your body in order by reaching out. You are one magnificent creator.

You deepen your healing process here as you fall in love a little deeper with all of life. It is part of falling in love with the process. It never ends. There is no "there" to get to. That's the magic, God bless you, indeed.

Y ou can ask God for assistance, but what you would want to ask is that the God that is you would come to the surface in its fullest expression.

And the only way that God can truly touch you and create such miracles as reversal of age, etc. is through, once again, immersing yourself in the absolute and utter belief, understanding and awareness that God is you and you are God.

Once you bring that to the surface, then everything in your life is in perfect harmony, and your physical body becomes a reflection of the absolutely beautiful, wondrous expression of self, this perfection of the universal, this perfection of God. And you will find that in an instant you can transform your physical reality.

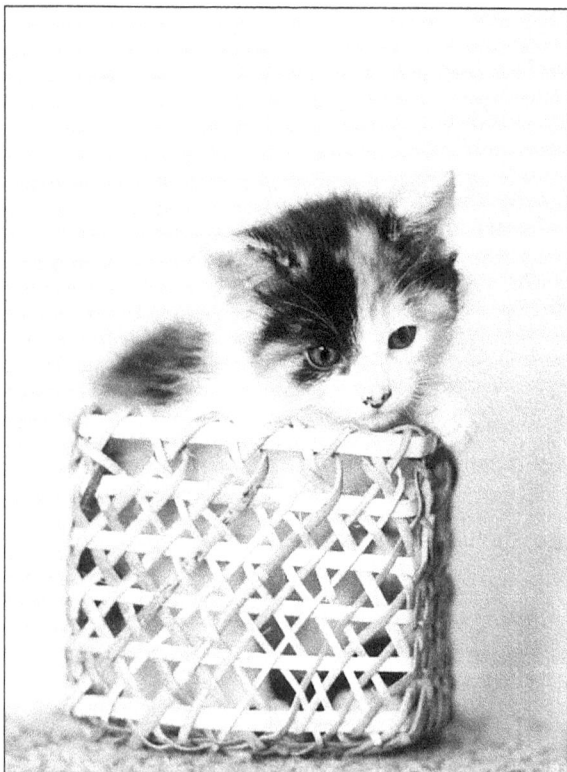

Kitten in Basket, Carlsbad, California

Pets

*

VH: Please tell us about our pets.

My dear friends, pets are unconditional lovers, and
they bring this to help us heal our hearts. This is the reason
they come. They have often been, at times, human in other
lifetimes. And in service to mankind they come back as
pets. Not all pets have been human; some have only chosen
to be pets.

> *M*y *dear friends, pets are truly the healers of
> the heart, for they love unconditionally in a
> way that people can receive.*

Pets do a beautiful job, for they expect nothing from
you but give much. God bless you, indeed.

VH: Do pets reincarnate with the same people at times?

God bless you, indeed. Very often, my dear. Some come
back as the same pet, with a different species, of course,
where they are around that person nonstop because they
have dedicated their lives to the helping of those individuals.
But that is not always the case. Other times, they choose to
be an animal and come into a certain family that can teach
them certain lessons.

So it is not so different, my dear, than it is with humans
who trade around different roles so they can learn about
other perspectives. They do that too, as well as being
of assistance.

Flowers

Abortion

‑ ✳ ‑

VH: *Please comment on abortion.*

Abortions, my dear, are also a choice. The being who chooses the parent … there is a great deal of knowingness ahead of time whether that parent will want that child or not. So the parent may choose to abort the baby, and all the child wanted was a feeling of what it felt like to be inside another human form.

W hen does the soul truly enter? Well, my dear, some enter at three months, some at six months, some actually during passage through the birth canal, and some three months after birth. The time is determined by the soul.

Sometimes a baby is born. The soul decided it wanted to take the body, but decided at the very last—for example, one month after birth—"Well, I don't think I want to do this one." The soul leaves, but leaves the body alive so a walk-in can come in and take it. But it is only sustained for so long, and it is usually around three months after birth that the body mechanics are maintained, because that is how long it has a life force coming from mother.

Oftentimes crib deaths and so on are because the soul chose not to come into the form. So it happens at all different times. There is no exact way that it is done.

Tree in Snow, Flagstaff, Arizona

Death

✳

VH: Please help us understand death.

*D*eath is dissolving that illusion of separation. It is opening the door, walking through and discovering who you really are, which is a very grand being.

So death is not an end to it all; it is a beginning—the beginning of knowing who you are, of joining all your fellow brothers and sisters in the kingdom of heaven.

When you pass over, the angels come and take you in their hands; they hold you and let you peek around!

The only problem when you pass over is holding on to this life. You leave the fear behind and there is nothing to fear, because there is just love on the other side!

It is not the final hour as beings often think of it. But it is a grand adventure, and we like to see it as opening the door and walking into a grand ballroom with people you know. Then you really begin the dance!

Young and Old, Central Mexico

Reincarnation

※

VH: Please explain reincarnation.

Reincarnation is when … well, there is no way that any one being could do it all right the first go-around. Reincarnation is the opportunity to continue to master oneself through many lifetimes.

I n coming back lifetime after lifetime, you master and claim the God that you are. This removes the veil so that you understand that we are all One. So it dissolves the illusion of separation.

Reincarnation is a wonderful thing that all of us on planet Earth agreed to take part in as a beautiful game. It is like playing baseball; you never play just one game. So you can liken it to a game. That is something you can understand, and that you just whet your appetite with only one game. Like that commercial that says you can't eat just one! (We're thinking of a potato chip!) One lifetime just whets your appetite, so to speak.

Stairway, Mexico

Suicide

※

VH: *Please comment on suicide.*

God bless you, indeed. That is a big subject, and carries much impact for many people.

S uicide is not condemned on this side by anyone, for it is an understanding that the soul decided that it could not quite make it and wanted a reprieve, so to speak.

However, once you do that, you don't get out of anything, for you must return to make up that lifetime and give back something for the life you took.

Everything is in agreement, and you agreed to come to the school called planet Earth and to fulfill a certain time period. So if you leave early, we embrace and love you, but you must return.

One thing you could liken this to is the child who runs out of the schoolroom and says, "I'm not going back, I've had it; I'm not doing math anymore!" You hold the child, you love the child, and you say, "My dear, but this is necessary for you in your life." So once you patch them up and help them to understand, then you send them back to the classroom again.

Old Barn with Square Nails, Northern California

Euthanasia

✳

VH: *Please comment on Euthanasia.*

Well, my dear, it is always a choice. It is a way for someone to leave the body by using a substance. However, there are many ways one can do it. You can do it by making the choice, "I am done. Now I choose to leave."

There is no judgment on this side, my dear, if a person uses a substance and has come to his last days. But there are many gifts that are often given in the final stages of dying.

We do not judge, so if this is the means that a person chooses to use, we will embrace and love that person. However, if there were lessons the soul had set up for those last stages of dying, then that person will have to correct it within the law of the universe. But there is no judgment on this side.

But if there was no lesson to learn in those last stages and a person chooses that course, then no corrections need be made. So, my dear, what it actually boils down to is that all souls must choose what feels right within their hearts. Only they know what they wish to do under those circumstances.

From this side, there is only loving allowance for all things to be, God bless you, indeed.

Seascape, Northern California

Donor Body Parts

✳

VH: What happens with the energy when one takes another person's body parts?

Well, my dear, this is also a choice. From our perspective here, if you take on another's body part, you take on that energy. So it is important for beings to understand that they are not just taking on a mechanical part, but they indeed are taking on a life force with it. If they choose to have a heart or something else transplanted, they need to know that the being who left that body will, in part, be with them.

So it is not a right or wrong, just a greater understanding that they may not be living in their body totally alone, God bless you, indeed.

The person donating the body part knows that ahead of time; they make that choice, do they not? So it is an agreement. You cannot take a human part unless the donation has been agreed before death. So there is an agreement there, and the party who wants that part is in agreement.

B *ut what is not understood is that they are taking on a part of that energy form—the soul of that being—especially in the case of a heart transplant.*

So we wouldn't say this so much just to enlighten people that the souls are all in agreement; there is no right or wrong. It is perfectly okay from our perspective, but understand that there is more at play here.

Squirrel with Bagel, Balboa Park, San Diego, California

Financial Security

✳

VH: *What can we do to help accomplish financial security?*

You could write a whole book on this particular subject matter, so it is going to be difficult to encapsulate this into a page or two. But we will try, God bless you, indeed.

Regarding financial security, there is none! That is it in a nutshell, my dear friends. To think of financial security is to build a false hope. There really is none, because in any moment in time it can be taken from you. When people say they want financial security, really what they are saying is that they want to know that their soul will be okay, that their beingness will be okay and will survive.

That is truly the crux of what they are saying when they are asking for financial security. They are just not realizing it. Or they think, "Well, if I have money in the bank, then I am okay." But how many beings have money in the bank and are not okay? A lot! And how many beings have no money in the bank, but trust the universe to provide what they need in each moment, yet live in peace, love and harmony? That is truly what the soul wants, to be able to create in the moment exactly what is needed.

*Y*ou can trust in the universe more by surrendering, my dear friends, by surrendering into the deeper, darker places within your soul and not being afraid to venture there.

S o, my dear friends, the dance to security is really the dance to your own hearts, feeling safe and secure and of value within yourselves.

When you have the serenity and security within you, all else follows suit. But for beings who are steeped in financial security, oftentimes what has eluded them is the security and peacefulness within themselves, and the money does them no good.

What you are really wanting, my dear friends—what the soul is really wanting—is to trust on a deeper level. One does this by surrendering, and it's a constant state of surrendering, and trust in the divineness of the Creator and the divineness of oneself. It is to know that you have the power to create all that you need in each and every moment. For some reason it has been portrayed that if you stockpile, much like a chipmunk would, you are going to be okay for whatever is to come. My dear friends, that is not where it is at.

W hat really brings about security is surrendering to Source and the power greater than you.

❋

Addiction

❋

VH: What can help a person regarding an addiction?

*W*hen you think about why somebody creates an addiction, it is only because they are afraid to see who they really are.

So they create something that will take them on a path away from who they are. But ultimately, it's going to take them back, because there's only so far you can go with an addiction before it slaps you right in the face.

Let's say you are walking down a path, and you can see something very beautiful and radiant at the end of the path. But as you looked at it, it scared you because you thought to yourself, "My goodness, what is that? Could that possibly be an E.T.? Could that possibly be God Himself? Could that possibly be …?" and you go on and on. Do you see what we are saying?

So you say, "Well, maybe if I take this path over here, I can go around the back of it and see it from another angle." So you take a path called addiction to the left and you go along this path. Sometimes you forget why you took it. You started on it because you wanted to see what that glow was, but you were afraid to come right up to it.

Then you take another path. Well, you get around to the back and you say, "Oh, my goodness, I can't quite see from this angle either." So ultimately you have to go back to the beginning point and start over. You take four more steps on the path and the light gets brighter yet. You get scared, so you take another path called addiction to deter you along the way, and you explore that for a while. But ultimately, my dear, all paths lead back to the center path, and you will find the light that you are. It is your fear of seeing who you really are, so you create addictions to mask that.

Chapel of the Holy Cross, Sedona, Arizona

Face of God

✳

VH: What do you mean exactly when you say 'face of God?'

When we talk about finding and touching the face of God, certainly this conjures up all kinds of images for you, and this is precisely what we want it to do. What does it make you think of first? Does it make you think of the Earth? Does it make you think of the universe? Does it make you think of an entity that exists somewhere outside of you? Does it make you think of an entity that exists somewhere inside of you? Does it make you think of your chair or another cup of coffee?

Doesn't matter: it is God. Doesn't matter what it conjures up for you; it is God. But when we share with you, my dear friends, that to search the darker spaces, to go into the darker colors, not fear them as the absence of light but rather understanding the darker colors as a density of the very same, you begin to understand you are no longer dividing yourself from the truth that is you, that is everything. All potential exists within you. All potential, all anger, all depression, all joy, all enlightenment, all growth, all opportunity—everything exists within you.

*S*o, my dear, you would take your hands and place them upon your face, and it is there that you find and touch the face of God.

But to truly do this, my dear friends, you journey to your heart, not holding any part of yourself at arm's length. You understand the experience of mere emotions to be something of opportunity, an opportunity for expression of self to the world, an opportunity for the world to express itself to you.

And so, my dear friends, it is a matter of what you choose to bring to the surface. For us, it is love, because doing anything else would not be doing what brings us joy. And to love you brings us tremendous joy. But, my dear friends, quite literally we mean the face of God that is you. Do you understand?

Mary Gunther, Virginia's Grandmother

Guides

✳

VH: I was considering packing away my numerous statues of Buddha when I had my house listed for sale. In a reading with Dr. Peebles, I received the following message.

Buddha is laughing loudly and inquiring, "Why would you want to get rid of statues of such a very beautiful, very wonderful, abundant, prosperous, generous, kind-hearted individual?" That would be Buddha, my dear, God bless you, indeed, expressing his heart's intent to you. He loves you very much. He has been around you, has been with you since you were a child.

He is a guide of yours and is also a part of our community of angels here.

VH: That's beautiful. (I'm crying.)

God bless you, indeed.

VH: And I can call on him?

Absolutely, my dear, he is never far away at all. You see? Now do you understand how it works? When you ask, my dear, you ask about names of guides, etc. And there are some who would prefer that you find it out on your own.

There is another, my dear. Are you not aware? Who else do you suppose would be a guide of yours?

VH: My grandmother?

Well, certainly, yes, without question. She loves you so much, my dear. She has graduated to great heights within her own soul.

S he is a very, very large spirit, and she does stand over you. You are not doing this alone at all, and we care very much about what happens with you and with your life.

She towers over you and gazes down upon you. She says she does this as part of standing very firm and tall to help propel you along your path, God bless you, indeed, when you cannot stand on your own two feet.

She says she is doing it for you, and she is the one who says, "Come on, little girl, put your chin up and move forward. We are not going to have any of this nonsense." She is a beautiful spirit and is around you.

VH: Are there certain books I can read to understand the life of Buddha?

His reply is "No." He would prefer for you to focus upon little idols sitting around in terms of statues, etc. The reason is because this is his preference.

B uddha wants to be remembered as one who is very round, very large, very abundant. Abundant in what, my dear? Abundant in joy, in celebration of life.

Why did he eat with a ravenous appetite? Because he had a tremendous appetite for life, a tremendous appetite for love. He wanted to take it all in. He knew he was one with everything, so he enjoyed his journey upon planet Earth with great grace. From our perspective, that is the word that encompasses him entirely. If you want to sum up his life in one word, it would be grace, because he is a very beautiful spirit, a very, very good partner of ours.

There is quite a family here, my dear. I function a little bit more as a spokesperson for a community of spirits who very much want to be heard. There is a communal voice. I have my certain reflections, opinions and perspectives.

A *nd part of my purpose in this communication is to bring forward my own spiritual psychology that I feel can help the planet in the people's own expression of heart to the world around them.*

Then, my dear, there are others: There is Joshua (known as Jesus), there is Buddha, there is Paramahansa Yogananda. There are other spirits, my dear friends, including an angel named Angela. There is one, a very beautiful companion of mine, who works in communication with Earth and is in training to come through many channels upon planet Earth in the future to continue my work. This is Harmony, a very beautiful, a very dear, dear friend of mine; and we work together continually in ongoing communication.

There are others within this family. There is Mack, the truck driver, who in his last life on planet Earth ate hamburgers and drove a truck. And he is one who works a little bit on the outskirts of the community, but he likes to throw in his two cents here and there. There is another beautiful Spirit known as Don Pendleton. And he is a very beautiful friend of ours. He wants very much to provide a little structure in lives upon planet Earth so within that structure they find autonomy and freedom.

And there are others. There is George who has been brought into the group as, what you would call upon planet Earth, one who is a gopher. One who goes for things, you see, who goes out to other dimensions to bring back information. He is a very good scout who works with us. He is in training here. He is going to reincarnate, but first he wants to work with us because we are working with the Channel, and he is a good friend of hers.

VH: I've heard the name George mentioned.

He is a beautiful Spirit. He communicates with you through wonderful, light-hearted wisdom and certainly through song. God bless you, indeed.

VH: When you said Harmony was in training to continue your work, does that mean you are going to stop?

At some time, my dear, yes. It is part of my great joy to continue work with planet Earth, a part of what I have planned but always can change. What is in my heart currently is that I will continue working with channels upon planet Earth as long as there are those who are willing to have me come through. I will be happy to assist. At some point, however, I am going to make a decision to tip my toes on planet Earth one more time just to celebrate me entirely throughout my life. And to enjoy the journey from beginning to end, as well to bring back others with me who would be functioning as family.

We are going to be doing some clean up upon planet Earth down the road a piece. But this is quite some time from now. God bless you, indeed. At that point we will be requiring someone to take over the work. We don't want to just leave planet Earth high and dry without a communicator. So Harmony is going to be doing the work there. She will be coming through before I complete my work and will begin to pop up here and there, but down the road a piece.

Fogged-In Grand Canyon, Arizona

A Craving For Sweets

*

VH: *Would you help me with my craving for sweets?*

Regarding a craving for sweets, some understanding as
to why you are gaining the weight in the first place would
be of assistance. But remember, my dear, you have just given
yourself permission to play, to indulge without shame—but
with curiosity—in the sweetness of life.

First of all, indulging in sweets and such, there is not a
problem at all. It's just a matter of enjoying it. When you
are feeling a desire to have a sweet, then you indulge immediately. The fastest you can respond to this craving that you
feel, the faster it will go. For example, you have on hand in
your pocket little pieces of chocolate all broken up, God bless
you, indeed. When you feel the craving, you pop one in and
you suck it, and you relish each and every single part of the
vibration of that sweetness. This will help you in tempering
your craving for the very same.

Similar effect, my dear, as to a homeopathic remedy. You
understand? It's okay, my dear; it's just a point whereby you
are bringing balance back to your body. But when you fight
it, when you resist it, God bless you, indeed, then you can't
resist anymore, and you lose all control. That's where you're
finding it becomes more of an addiction.

G *iving yourself permission can work wonders in
all kinds of ways.*

Lactose Intolerance

※

For those individuals who would prefer to receive benefits from such things as milk, cheese, yogurt, for example …

> …you would simply, for those who have an inability to digest milk, understand that this is a response here to having a lack of nurturing as a child, lack of mommy's milk. Being pushed away by the very same creates what is known as lactose intolerance.

So how do they bridge this without fancy drugs and pills, without taking themselves away from that which they cherish and love and truly need as a process of healing and understanding within themselves of nurturing?

Well, you take a glass of milk and you have a little sniff. You ask this milk to agree with your tummy. It is the very same effect as a homeopathic remedy. Simply sniffing the milk before you drink it would help the digestive enzymes fall into place in a much better, stronger fashion within the tummy. The very same with smelling cheese or eggs and taking a bite—not cooked, however. Smell the raw egg first.

This is more a matter of connecting with your food and helping to settle responses within. Take care in this territory, however, because this can set a stage of expectation regarding allergies of various kinds. You must do it with real, true intent, setting the stage within your body. You sniff the milk and create responses in your physical body.

Simply sniffing milk is not going to create the response; it is the desire that creates the response, the manufacturing of properties that will help to digest the various foods to ensure that the individual will not be allergic. Yes, and remember if you are allergic to it, there is going to be a tendency not to like the smell.

Solstice, Machu Picchu, Peru

Community

✳

VH: *What do you mean when you recommend that people be in community?*

There are many levels to feeling a part of community. To be in community can mean to be in the physical community.

*T*o be in community too, my dear, as you open up to who you are, you are in community to help others do the same.

When you stay within the illusion of separation, my dear, within yourself, you stay isolated from community. When you stay isolated on a piece of property, in a way you are in the physical staying isolated. One is on the physical and the other is on the spiritual-emotional level.

Grandmother & Baby, Lake Patzcuaro, Mexico

Appendix

The three principles are given in greater detail by Dr. Peebles:

Principle #1
Loving Allowance

✳

L oving allowance for ALL things to be in their own time and place, starting with YOURSELF.

God bless you, indeed. Emphasize "all" and "yourself." My dear friends, loving allowance for all things to be in their own time and place. This is something that you don't want to control, do you? Truly? Do you want the responsibility of controlling everything around you? No, not at all, my dear friends. Surrender and have loving allowance for all things to be in their own time and place, starting with yourself.

Do you want to be in the chains you have kept yourself in? Do you want to have the control within you? Do you want to slap yourself every time you try to speak? Do you want to tell yourself that you are no longer worthy, that you are not worth attention, that you are not worth coming to the surface, that your opinions and your voice do not count? Do you want to make these sorts of decisions about yourself? God bless you, indeed.

We believe here that within your heart of hearts you would say to us, "No," and that you would rather have loving allowance for all things to be in their own time and place, starting with yourself.

A llow yourself to speak your truth, allow yourself to come to the surface, allow yourself to be admired, allow yourself to be loved, allow yourself, my dear friends, to express yourselves with confidence, with trust, with love, with generosity of spirit.

Would you, my dear friends, consider yourselves to be giving? My dear friends, we would have to say, from our perspective, only approximately 50% of the time. Because, my dear friends, how often do you not give of yourself? It is not what you give. It is not in the form of money, in the form of a gift, it is not in the form of the work you do. It is, my dear friends, in terms of the love you choose to give to the world. This love takes many forms.

I f you want to love the world, then, my dear friends, you will give to the world of yourself, no matter what color or shape or size that takes.

And you do it, my dear friends, with respect, increasing your communication with the world around you sharing of yourself. This, my dear friends, helps others to fly free, because now they understand you; now the unspoken truths become spoken truths. Now, my dear friends, the sharing, the intimacy begins, the contact occurs. This is absolute and true love.

T his is where you find that the journey to your own heart is one of adventure and fascination.

It is where you find the abundance, the richness, the rewards that come with a sense of discovery about you.

You can struggle to hold yourselves at arm's length if you like! You can do it now in this lifetime, but we are going to send you right back to planet Earth. Or, my dear friends, you can allow yourself to have contact within—within your own heart—and understand that the learning and discoveries about you never end. It is here, my dear, that indeed, Virginia, you do find and touch the face of God.

And it is here, my dear friends, that you discover the reason you feel restless, the reason you feel confused, is that your soul wants to move, your soul wants to be free, your soul wants to be expressed. Your soul does not want to be denied anymore. And, God bless you, indeed, you begin to shift this energy, because you are beautiful and loving human beings. Do you not care about everyone with sincerity? My dear friends, to a point, yes. But you care about yourself.

N ow express your truth to the world, and in honoring yourself in this fashion, you are honoring "all" of creation. Would you understand, my dear friends?

Storytelling Time, Culver City, California

Principle #2
Increase Communication With All of Life

✳

*I*ncrease communication with all of life, starting with YOURSELF, and with respect.

So now, my dear friends, you have explored loving allowance for all things to be in their own time and place, starting with yourself!

Loving allowance for me to be, God bless you, indeed, today in my wholeness, in my completeness, in my very beautiful heart.

And it is here I celebrate myself by sharing with you, with permission, of course. And increasing communication with respect here so we can embark upon a beautiful dance, a journey, a labor of love, a journey to our own heart, a deepening and widening and broadening and expansion here of our consciousness together, God bless you, indeed.

Girl on Swing, Los Angeles, California

Principle #3
Self-Responsibility for Your Life

✳

*S*elf-responsibility for your life as a creative
*adventure, for through your choices and
perceptions, you do indeed create your reality. And
never in your eternal soul have you been a victim but
always the creator.*

Self-responsibility for your life as a creative adventure, for
through your choices and perceptions, you do indeed create
your reality, my dear friends. We ask for you to start each
day with this principle. Change the statement just a wee bit,
and share it with yourself in the mirror:

"Self-responsibility for my life as a creative adventure, for
through my choices and perceptions I do indeed create my
reality. And never in my eternal soul have I been a victim,
but always the creator."

You do this each and every morning, my dear friends.
Why die in wonderment at you, the reflection of you in the
mirror, speaking the words to self in harmony?

*Y*ou will find that with each passing day, your
*heart will be glistening, glistening with gold,
prosperous and abundant beings that you are, coming
to the surface, abundant with choices, abundant with
perceptions, abundant because you, my dear friends,
are the creators, not the victims.*

And it is here, my dear friends, when you listen to yourself, your own heartbeat, you will begin to understand how it beats in harmony with the world. And you no longer fear bringing more of yourself to the surface, to the expression of your soul, God bless you, indeed.

(Dr. Peebles always ends his sessions with the following:)

My dear friends, go your way in peace, love and harmony, for life is indeed a joy, and all you have to do is enjoy the journey to your own hearts, and certainly to your own enlightenment; you simply lighten up just a little bit more, God bless you, indeed.

Mileposts on A Journey to Your Heart

✵

God bless you, indeed, Dr. Peebles here. It is a joy and a blessing when man and spirit join together in search of the greater truths and awareness. (P. 3)

My dear friends, the process upon planet Earth is a process of understanding your own hearts, releasing yourself from the constraints here of your mind and understanding how to speak the language of the heart using the mind as a tool rather than an expression itself. (P. 5)

In order to explore this, your guides have created a beautiful school, they said, a beautiful school called planet Earth. It looks rather amazing from a distance, a beautiful blue orb here floating out in the universe, out in the center of this darkness. (P. 6)

God bless you, indeed, you come closer and closer, and as you do, you begin to pass through an area called the Valley of Forgetfulness where you forget where you were in the universe. (P. 7)

 ${Y}$ ou begin to realize how you are a part of this Earth, how every thought, every deed that you create here has a resonance. And, my dear friends, the only purpose for you upon the Earth is to immerse yourself in life. (P. 8)

 ${Y}$ ou, my dear friends, are the paintbrush. Planet Earth is your canvas. And your heart that comes from God, my dear friends, is the paint with which you color it. (P. 8)

 ${L}$ ife is a dance, my dear friends. Everything that occurs around you has value, has purpose. There is not one single solitary bit of life here upon Earth that you would ever want to push away. (P. 10)

...the learning never ever ends; it spirals out now and forevermore, and it is there that you continue in an ongoing exploration of God. (P. 10)

 ${W}$ hen you cross the threshold, it is there that you feel consciousness of love for everything and everyone. (P. 11)

 ${M}$ y dear friends, there is passion to be found in every single, solitary corner of the universe. (P. 11)

...and how life is so beautiful because it provides you with a basis of understanding the honest echo that you receive in return. (P. 12)

*B*ut, my dear friends, fall in love with your heart. Journey therein and you will find contact there, and it will continue and spiral out forevermore, God bless you, indeed. (P. 12)

*T*apping your chest, you can say that a few ways. "Teach my mind today, heart. Teach my mind today, heart. Teach my mind today, heart. Today, heart, teach my mind." (P. 12)

*Y*ou can sit each day and make a list of all the things you are grateful for and feel them within your heart. (P. 15)

*T*ake big deep breaths each day, my dear friends, and breathe deeply. And as you breathe in life and you breathe out, you release all that does not belong there. (P. 15)

*Y*ou can focus your attention and love upon Mother Earth, your awareness of planet Earth. As you step upon her, you give her love and understand that you put your resonance into her. (P. 19)

*E*verything is fine, my dear friends, nothing to fear, but to understand it is certainly a process whereby planet Earth is moving into a new dimension, a greater frequency. (P. 19)

*C*ertainly God that you are, for you are God and God is you. (P. 20)

*A*nd it is here that you deepen your awareness of self in relationship to life as you learn to embrace all the extremes and the extension of self, God bless you, indeed, and all the spectrums of light and life within you, my dear friends. (P. 20)

*A*nd you do have the capability of changing and transforming the energy of planet Earth, of changing what you see as the possible end of the world, if you will. (P. 21)

*I*t is a time of growth and opportunity for everyone, unimaginable opportunity for expression of compassion, expression of your individuality. (P. 22)

*L*et go of the "there" to get to and simply surrender to your heart. That is where you will create movement in your life. (P. 23)

*A*nd you will find you are surrendering to the will of the universe. That is what is for your highest good. (P. 23)

*M*ost fatigue is because people are not honoring themselves and they are not taking time to do what makes their hearts sing. (P. 25)

$\mathcal{B}$ut, my dear, truly it is about becoming the God you are and dissolving the illusion of separation. When you dissolve the illusion of separation and become the best you can be, it sets up a chain reaction within the universe for others to do the same. (P. 30)

$\mathcal{T}$ouch is so very important, my dear. When you are touched, one God is touching the next God and through that, healing occurs. So without touch, life does not survive. (P. 33)

$\mathcal{T}$here are many things that man does not know about as far as how deeply this goes. It is soul touching soul. It is memory touching memory when we were all as One. (P. 33)

$\mathcal{S}$o it does away with the pedestal upon which the great ascended masters and God have been placed, my dear friends, for we are all Gods and we are all One. (P. 34)

$\mathcal{W}$e are connected to a divine power source, and it travels through the different layers of our etheric bodies and to our human body and circulates around our body. (P. 36)

$\mathcal{T}$here is no such thing as "the" religion, for all religions have truth, and as long as a religion teaches Divine love, it is the right path for that being. (P. 39)

$\mathcal{A}$ change in time is setting things on course. You've also heard about the magnetic pole exchange, where there is no north and south. The planet is making shifts in that way, and there is a change in time affecting that. (P. 41)

$\mathcal{I}$n thinking about aging, my dear friends, you don't get older unless you choose to get older. (P. 45)

$\mathcal{W}$ell, my dear friends, relationships weren't designed to be smooth. They were designed to help us perfect ourselves. So it is a bit of a paradox here. (P. 49)

$\mathcal{R}$elationships truly are the dance to your own soul. It is a way to be in touch with all the parts of yourself that you cannot see. (P. 50)

$\mathcal{A}$nd through the dance of harmony, you learn to dance in harmony with Spirit. So it is a mirroring of the heavens too within the relationship dance upon the Earth. (P. 50)

$\mathcal{A}$nd when you are a seeker of the greater truths, you are a seeker of understanding here, you are a seeker of healing, you are a seeker of compassion, and so on and so forth, my dear friends. (P. 52)

$\mathcal{A}$nd, God bless you indeed, that is where the struggle begins, my dear. That is where you learn about true love, absolute love. (P. 53)

So let go of any "there" you want to get to and realize that this process you are engaged in, in terms of surrender, is certainly an awakening of your heart. (P. 54)

You are only a portion, my dear, of who you really are. You are not all of you, for there are other aspects of you out experiencing different things to bring back to the whole. (P. 57)

In the relationship of human sexuality to the Divine, yes, certainly you can reach enlightenment upon the planet Earth. (P. 59)

But for ultimate divine satisfaction, if you will, to engage with one person, one individual, one-on-one contact is best. (P. 60)

When you come into this state of bliss, my dear, there is no separation between male and female or bad and good or right and wrong. God bless you, indeed. It is all One. It is a state of oneness. (P. 60)

The problems that come about, in terms of human sexuality, come through a belief in arm's length—certainly through thoughts of shame and guilt and so on. (P. 61)

*B*ut my dear friends, you understand that to truly fall in love with the state of oneness, that consciousness, you need to realize in celebration of self that everything exists within you, and that within every man, within every woman and within every child exists an Enlightened Being. (P. 62)

*I*f you can learn to love one person, to see yourself reflected in that person fully, and to learn about yourself; if you can fall in love with the exploration of self in relationship to this person, then you will find your enlightenment, because you are falling in love with "you." (P. 63)

*W*e want you to explore life, to find yourself in love with everything. Because, my dear, if you can imagine for a moment that you are God … does God, my dear, push away any of life? (P. 63)

*W*ell, it is as we look upon time, my dear. The past, the present and the future we can see the same as if you were looking at the city from an airplane. (P. 65)

*B*ut it is all occurring at the same time. Because we don't have time like you think of it. The soul evolves quite rapidly upon Earth and your time is only a flicker here. (P. 66)

*Y*ou begin to understand that anger is a force that creates movement within your life. (P. 67)

$\mathcal{B}$ut indeed, my dear friends, anger is a momentum, a force, getting out of an energy that has trapped a thought process within you where you felt you had no say. (P. 68)

$\mathcal{B}$ecause, my dear friends, the balance that you truly seek is within your own spirit, within your own soul. (P. 69)

$\mathcal{Y}$ou keep your body in order by reaching out. You are one magnificent creator. (P. 71)

$\mathcal{Y}$ou can ask God for assistance, but what you would want to ask is that the God that is you would come to the surface in its fullest expression. (P. 71)

$\mathcal{M}$y dear friends, pets are truly the healers of the heart for they love unconditionally in a way that people can receive. (P. 73)

$\mathcal{W}$hen does the soul truly enter? Well, my dear, some enter at three months, some at six months, some actually during passage through the birth canal, and some three months after birth. The time is determined by the soul. (P. 75)

$\mathcal{D}$eath is dissolving that illusion of separation. It is opening the door, walking through and discovering who you really are, which is a very grand being. (P. 77)

*I*n coming back lifetime after lifetime, you master and claim the God that you are. This removes the veil so that you understand that we are all One. So it dissolves the illusion of separation. (P. 79)

*S*uicide is not condemned on this side by anyone, for it is an understanding that the soul decided that it could not quite make it and wanted a reprieve, so to speak. (P. 81)

*T*here is no judgment on this side, my dear, if a person uses a substance and has come to his last days. But there are many gifts that are often given in the final stages of death. (P. 83)

*B*ut what is not understood is that they are taking on a part of that energy form—the soul of that being—especially in the case of a heart transplant. (P. 85)

*Y*ou can trust in the universe more by surrendering, my dear friends, by surrendering into the deeper, darker places within your soul and not being afraid to venture there. (P. 87)

*S*o, my dear friends, the dance to security is really the dance to your own hearts, feeling safe and secure and of value within yourselves. (P. 88)

*W*hat really brings about security is surrendering to Source and the power greater than you. (P. 88)

When you think about why somebody creates an addiction, it is only because they are afraid to see who they really are. (P. 90)

So, my dear, you would take your hands and place them upon your face, and it is there that you find and touch the face of God. (P. 93)

She is a very, very large spirit, and she does stand over you. You are not doing this alone at all, and we care very much about what happens with you and with your life. (P. 98)

Buddha wants to be remembered as one who is very round, very large, very abundant. Abundant in what, my dear? Abundant in joy, in celebration of life. (P. 98)

And part of my purpose in this communication is to bring forward my own spiritual psychology that I feel can help the planet in the people's own expression of heart to the world around them. (P. 99)

Giving yourself permission can work wonders in all kinds of ways. (P. 103)

...you would simply for those who have an inability to digest milk, understand that this is a response here to having a lack of nurturing as a child, lack of mommy's milk. Being pushed away by the very same creates what is known as lactose intolerance. (P. 104)

*T*o be in community too, my dear, as you open up to who you are, you are in community to help others do the same. (P. 107)

*L*oving allowance for all things to be in their own time and place, starting with yourself. (P. 109)

*A*llow yourself to speak your truth, allow yourself to come to the surface, allow yourself to be admired, allow yourself to be loved, allow yourself, my dear friends, to express yourselves with confidence, with trust, with love, with generosity of spirit. (P. 110)

*I*f you want to love the world, then, my dear friends, you will give to the world of yourself, no matter what color or shape or size that takes. (P. 110)

*N*ow express your truth to the world, and in honoring yourself in this fashion, you are honoring "all" of creation. Would you understand, my dear friends? (P. 111)

*T*his is where you find that the journey to your own heart is one of adventure and fascination. (P. 111)

*I*ncrease communication with all of life, starting with yourself, and with respect. (P. 113)

*S*elf-responsibility for your life as a creative adventure, for through your choices and perceptions, you do indeed create your reality. And never in your eternal soul have you been a victim but always the creator. (P. 115)

*Y*ou will find that with each passing day, your heart will be glistening, glistening with gold, prosperous and abundant beings that you are, coming to the surface, abundant with choices, abundant with perceptions, abundant because you, my dear friends, are the creators, not the victims. (P. 115)

*M*y dear friends, go your way in peace, love and harmony, for life is indeed a joy, and all you have to do is enjoy the journey to your own hearts, and certainly to your own enlightenment; you simply lighten up just a little bit more, God bless you, indeed. (P. 116)

About Virginia Harford

*

A California native, Virginia now lives in San Miguel de Allende, Guanajuato, Mexico. Her background includes an Associate in Arts Degree in Recreational Leadership and a Bachelor of Science Degree in Physical Education from UCLA (University of California at Los Angeles).

She has had careers in business and education: as a dress buyer for a national retailer in Los Angeles and teaching ESL (English as a Second Language) in elementary through college levels. Virginia taught gentle exercises, breathing techniques and an accredited course of T'ai Chi Chih at Yavapai Retirement College in Arizona. She also instructed Chi Kung movements in Sedona, Arizona, San Diego, California, New Hampshire, Rio Caliente Spa near Guadalajara, Mexico, and San Miguel de Allende, Mexico, in 2013 and 2014. Virginia taught the first class of T'ai Chi Chih at the T'ai Chih Chih Center in Albuquerque when it opened in 1993.

Health and wellness have held a consistent and special interest for her, leading to Certification in Jin Shin Jyutsu (Acupressure), Reflexology, Rebirthing, Reiki and completing a year's program in Physical Fitness and Health Management from the University of California, San Diego at La Jolla. While in Europe, she attended the Sebastian Kneipp School, Bad Worishofen, Germany and obtained a Certificate in Introduction to Kneipp Physiotherapie and Spa Treatments. In Sedona, she studied gentle Chi Kung movements for longevity followed by becoming a certified teacher of T'ai Chi Chih in 1992. While living in New

Mexico, she joined a group of T'ai Chi teachers meeting at Justin Stone's home for weekly practice. Justin was the creator of T'ai Chi Chih.

Virginia has visited many countries. She took a five-month trip around the world at one time, visiting Europe, India and the Orient. During three months, she visited many spa towns in Europe, then spent a month at an Indian ashram, and concluded with a return visit after twenty-five years to Kyoto, Japan. She also spent two weeks on a memorable trip to Peru. She continues to explore Mexico, her new home.

Virginia Harford

Three Principles

✳

1. *Loving allowance for **all** things to be in their own time and place, starting with **yourself**.*

2. *Increase communication with all of life, starting with **yourself**, and with respect.*

3. *Self-responsibility for **my** life as a creative adventure, for through **my** choices and perceptions I do indeed create **my** reality. And never in my eternal soul have I been a victim, but always the creator.*

This is the creed of Dr. James Martin Peebles.
(It can be framed or placed on the mirror.)

www.ingramcontent.com/pod-product-compliance
Lightning Source LLC
Chambersburg PA
CBHW071451070426
42452CB00039B/1078